Note: If your learner knows the beginning consonant sounds and can read one of the words in the list, he/she will be able to read most or all of the words in that family.

Read these word families.

at	**et**	**in**	**ot**	**un**
bat	bet	bin	cot	bun
cat	get	fin	dot	fun
fat	jet	kin	got	gun
hat	let	pin	hot	nun
mat	met	sin	lot	run
Nat	pet	tin	not	sun
pat	set	win	pot	
rat	vet		rot	
sat	wet		tot	
vat				

I read these word families to ________________.

Read the Words

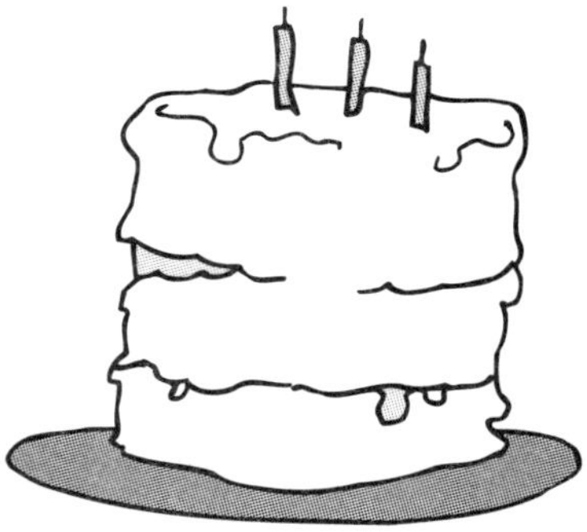

cake

snake

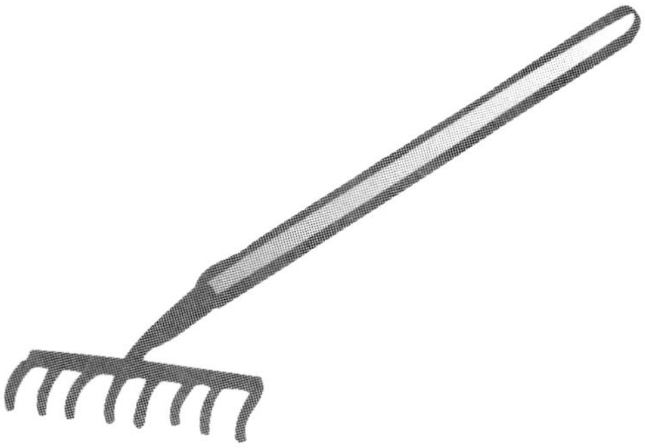

rake

bake

cake

fake

lake

make

quake

rake

take

wake

brake

shake

snake

I read these words to ________________.

Write the name of the picture on the line.

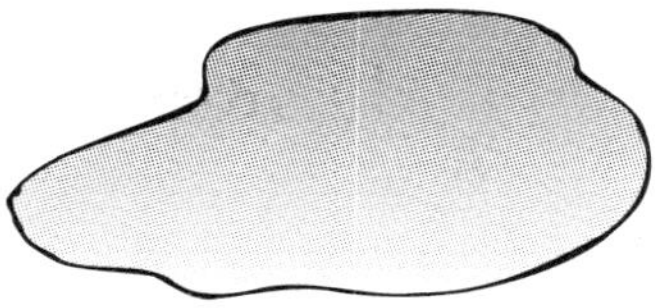

lake ______________

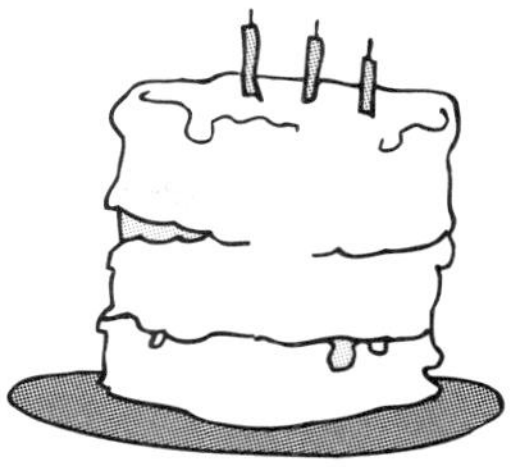

____

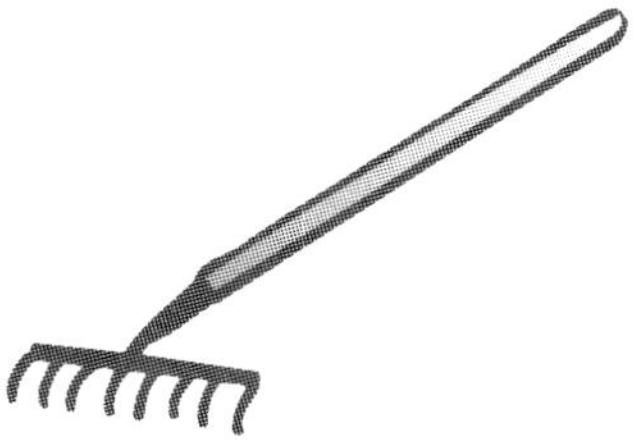

____

____

Fill in the blanks.

1. Dad will bake______ a c______ for my birthday.

2. I had to sh______ the bed to w______ my sister.

3. Did you find that sn______ at the l______?

I read these sentences to ______________.

Read the story.
Circle words that rhyme with <u>bake</u>.

Jake's Snake

Jake went to rake the backyard.

"Dad, Dad!" yelled Jake.
"Come here."

Dad ran to the backyard.
"What is it?" he asked.

Jake poked at a bush with the rake.
"I see a snake in that bush," he said.

"Don't shake the bush, Jake.
Let the snake alone.
It will go away when it wakes up."

I read this story to _______________.

Note: Your learner may need help reading the special words on this page.

yard yelled poked alone away

Read the Words

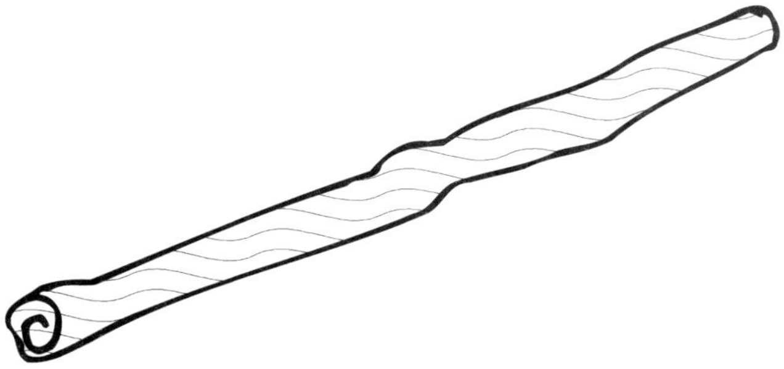

stick

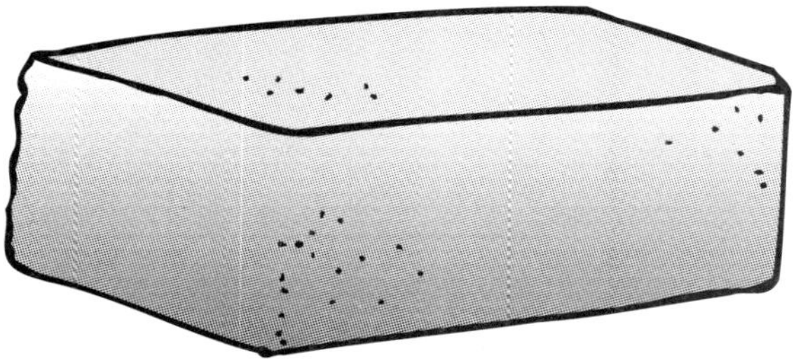

brick

chick

kick

quick

brick

stick

lick

sick

chick

thick

pick

tick

click

trick

I read these words to ________________.

Write the name of the picture on the line.

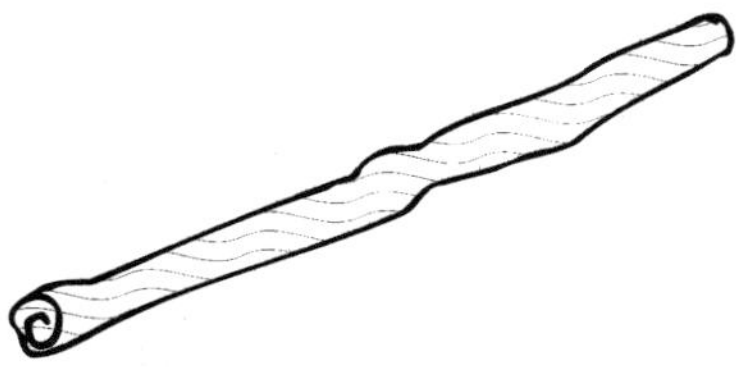

stick

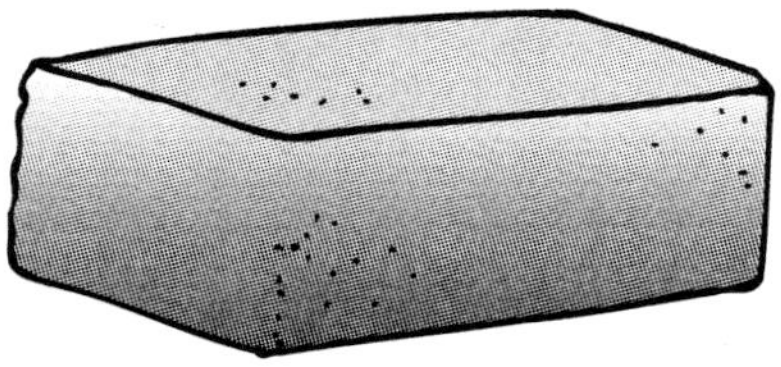

Fill in the blanks.

1. Can you kick the ball to the br________ wall?

2. Nick did a qu________ tr________.

3. P________ up that th________ st________.

I read these sentences to ________________.

Start at 1.
Connect the dots.

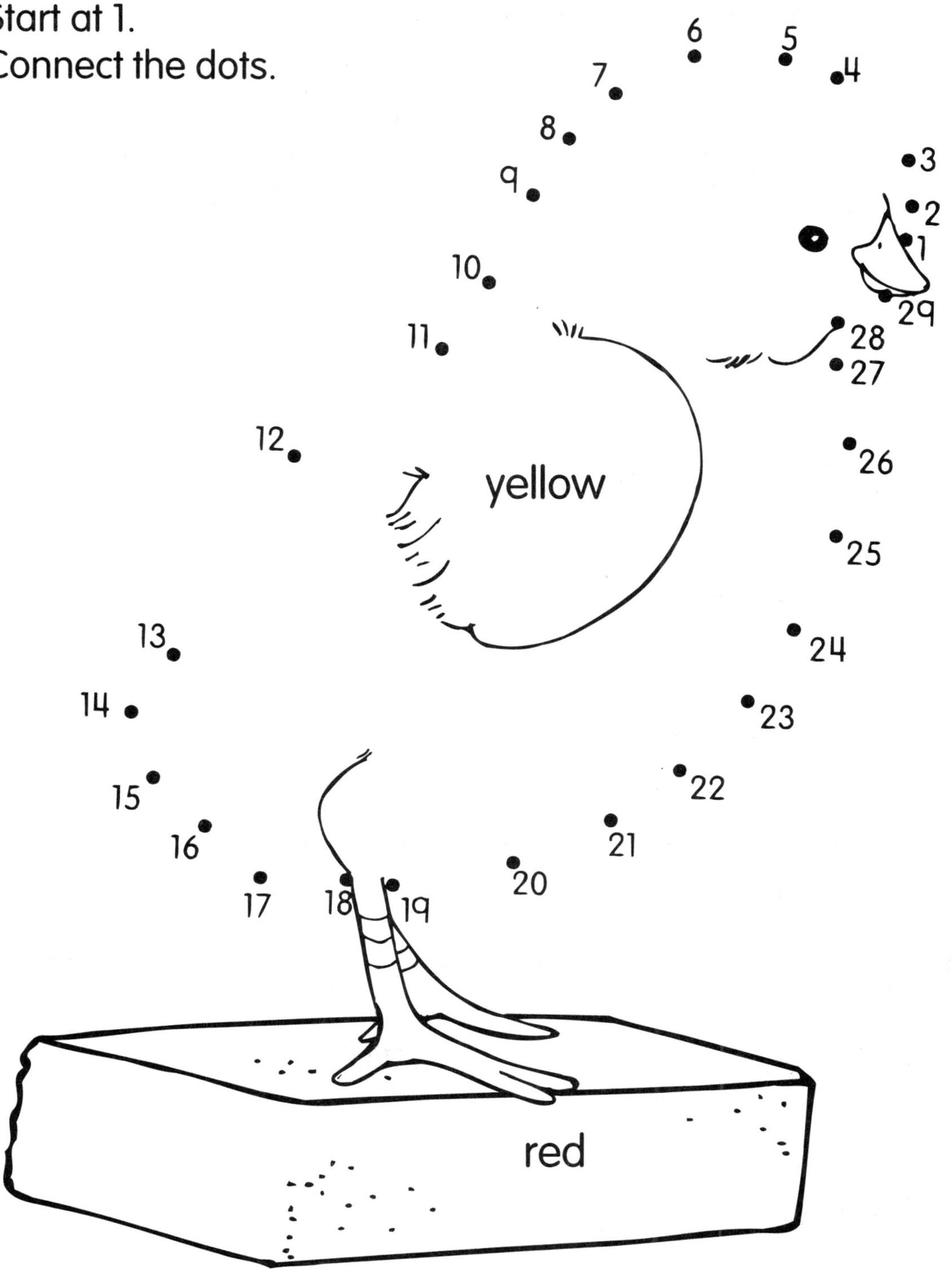

What did you make?

a yellow ____________________

on a red ____________________

Read the story.
Put a line under words that rhyme with kick.

Nick's Chick

Nick was sick.
He had to stay in bed.

Mom got Nick a trick chick on a stick.
The chick went "click, click, click"
as it ran up and down the stick.

The funny chick made Nick feel better.

I read this story to ________________.

Note: Your learner may need help reading the special words on this page.

stay funny better down feel

Read the Words

clown

gown

crown

down

brown

drown

gown

clown

frown

town

crown

I read these words to ________________.

Write the name of the picture on the line.

crown ____________

____

____

____

Fill in the blanks.

1. She had a rip in her yellow gown____________.

2. The cl____________ did tricks with a br____________ dog.

3. The king went d____________ t____________ to get his cr____________.

I read these sentences to ____________.

Read the story.
Put an X on the words that rhyme with down.

The Sad King

"The king is not happy.
See that big frown.
What can we do to make him smile?"
asked the queen.

"I saw a clown when I was downtown,"
said the prince.
We can get her to make the king smile."

The clown came in a funny, brown gown.
She did tricks for the king.

"I will not frown now," said the king.
"I like the tricks you did."
And the king gave the clown his crown.

I read this story to ________________.

Note: Your learner may need help reading the special words on this page.

happy smile asked prince king queen

Read the Words

ball

wall

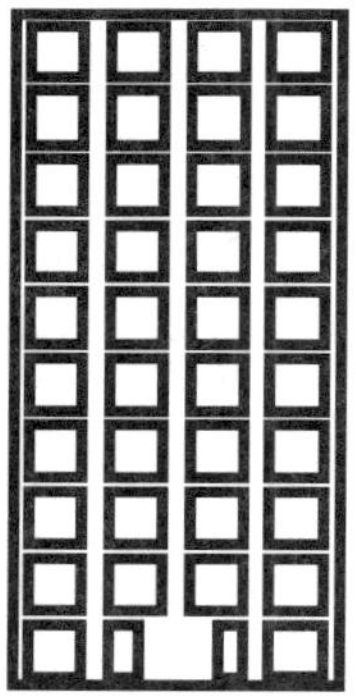

tall

ball

hall

wall

call

mall

small

fall

tall

stall

I read these words to ________________.

Write the name of the picture on the line.

small ________________

____

____

____

Fill in the blanks.

1. Pam ran to get the sm__________ b__________.

2. Do not f__________ off the t__________ w__________.

3. C__________ Mom and see if you can go to the m__________.

I read these sentences to ________________.

Read and Draw

six small balls

a tall brick wall

Read the story.
Look for the words that rhyme with all.

The Best Gift

Kate went to the mall to get a gift for her small brother.
She was looking for the best gift.

Kate looked in each stall up and down the hall.
She went in and out of the toy and gift shops.

At last she gave a big call, "I will get him that ball!
He will like to bounce it on the tall wall at the park."

Write the words in the story that rhyme with all.

mall ____________ ____________

____________ ____________

____________ ____________

____________ ____________

I read this story to ________________.

Note: Your learner may need help reading the special words on this page.

brother toy bounce looked gift shops

Read the Words

jay

hay

gray

bay
jay
pay
way
gray
today
day
lay
ray
bray
play
stay
hay
may
say
clay
pray
tray

I read these words to _______________.

Write the name of the picture on the line.

jay ____________

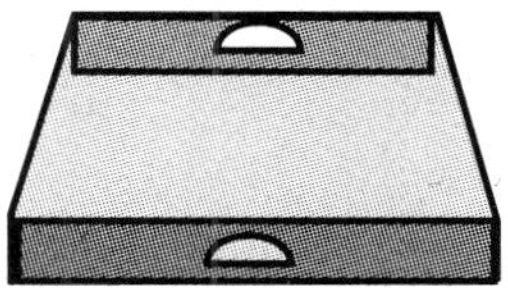

____

____

____

Fill in the blanks.

1. Ray made a jay __________ out of c l __________.

2. Will you st __________ and
   p l __________ with me?

3. I saw a g r __________ whale in the b __________ .

I read these sentences to ________________.

Read the story.
Put a circle around the words that rhyme with day.

A Gray (Jay)

Jay wanted to go out and play.
It was a cold, gray day.
"You have to stay inside today," said his mother.

Jay sat and looked outside.
He saw a blue jay in the tree.
"I will make that jay with my clay," he said.

He did not have blue clay so he made a gray jay.
"That is just the way I want it to look," said Jay.

Just then a ray of sunshine came in.
"You can go out now," called his mother.

Jay put the gray jay on a tray.
He set it on his desk.
He ran out into the sunshine to play.

I read this story to ________________.

Note: Your learner may need help reading the special words on this page.

wanted inside sunshine cold outside looked

Read the Words

cry

spy

fly

by

dry

shy

why

my

fly

sky

spy

cry

fry

try

I read these words to ____________________.

Write the name of the picture on the line.

sky ____________

____

____

____

Fill in the blanks.

1. Why ________ is he so sh ____________?

2. Can you fl ____________ your kite in the sk ____________?

3. Don't cr ____________. I will tr ____________ to help you.

I read these sentences to ____________.

Start at 1.
Connect the dots.

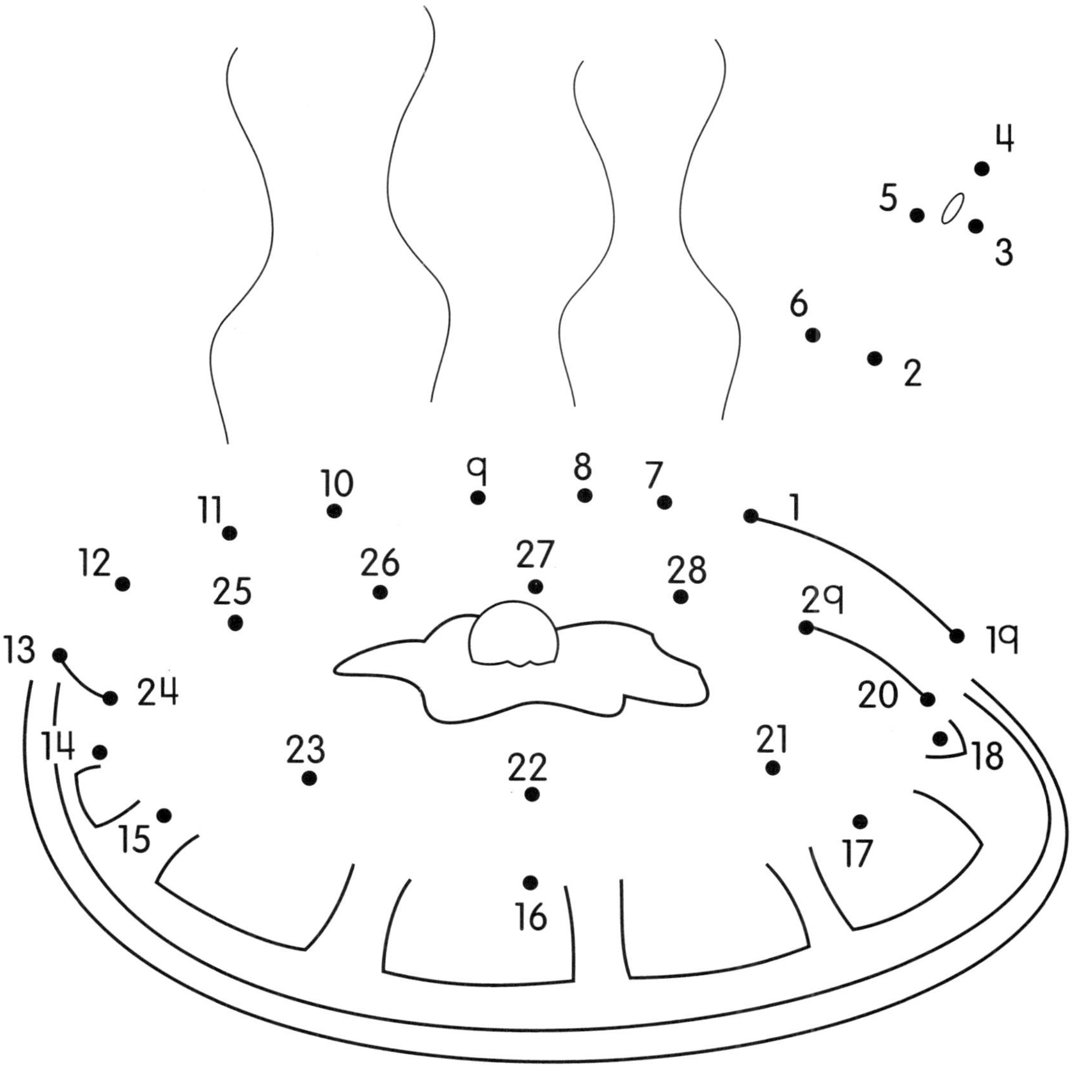

What do you see?

an ________________ in a _______________ing pan

Read the story.
Put an X on all of the words that rhyme with <u>my</u>.

Up in a Tree

The small boy wanted to fly his plane.
"I will try to get it up in the sky," he said.
He saw the plane fly. Then it hit a tree.
He started to cry.

A big girl came by. "Don't cry," she said.
"I will try to get the plane."
She went up the tree and got the plane.

"Here it is," she said.
"Why don't you fly it away from the tree."

"Thank you," said the shy boy.

I read this story to ________________.

Note: Your learner may need help reading the special words on this page.
wanted Don't from started away thank

Read the Words

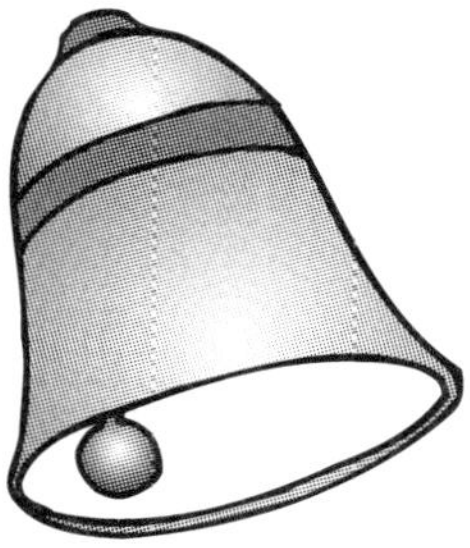

bell

well

shell

bell

tell

shell

fell

well

smell

sell

yell

spell

I read these words to ____________________.

Write the name of the picture on the line.

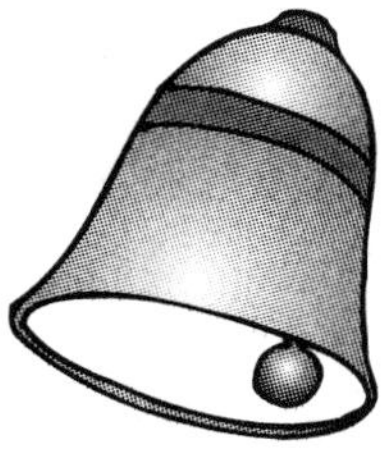

______________ ______________

____

Fill in the blanks.

1. Yell______ when you sm______ the cake.

2. Can you sp______ sh______?

3. The b______ f______ down the w______.

I read these sentences to ______________.

Read the story.
Circle the words that rhyme with bell.

What a Smell!

Ring the bell.
Give a yell.
Run and tell.
A skunk just squirted my pup.

Mr. Fell,
What do you sell
To get rid of the smell?
Can you clean him up?

I read this story to ________________.

Note: Your learner may need help reading the special words on this page.

squirted clean give Mr.

Read the Words

light

night

knight

fight
night
sight
flight
light
knight
tight
fright
might
right
bright
tonight

I read these words to ________________.

Write the name of the picture on the line.

____

____

____

Fill in the blanks.

1. Todd saw a bright__________

l__________ last n__________.

2. Is it r__________ to get in a f__________?

3. The plane fl__________

will start r__________ here.

I read these sentences to __________.

Read and Draw

knights in a fight

a bright light

a dark night

Read the story.
Put an X on the words that rhyme with light.

A Fright in the Night

A knight was going back to the castle.
It was very late on a very dark night.
Suddenly he saw a bright light far off.
"What was that?" he said.
"I must get closer so I can see."

The knight got a bad fright.
The light had come from a huge dragon.
"What am I going to do?" said the knight.
"I don't want to fight a dragon tonight."

Just then the dragon took flight.
The knight did not have to fight that night.

I read this story to ________________.

Note: Your learner may need help reading the special words on this page.

castle closer took huge suddenly dragon

Write Rhyming Words

cake rake make

sick

down

ball

may

fly

back

ball

night

Answer Key

Please take time to go over the work your child has completed. Ask your child to explain what he/she has done. Praise both success and effort. If mistakes have been made, explain what the answer should have been and how to find it. Let your child know that mistakes are a part of learning. The time you spend with your child helps let him/her know you feel learning is important.

page 3

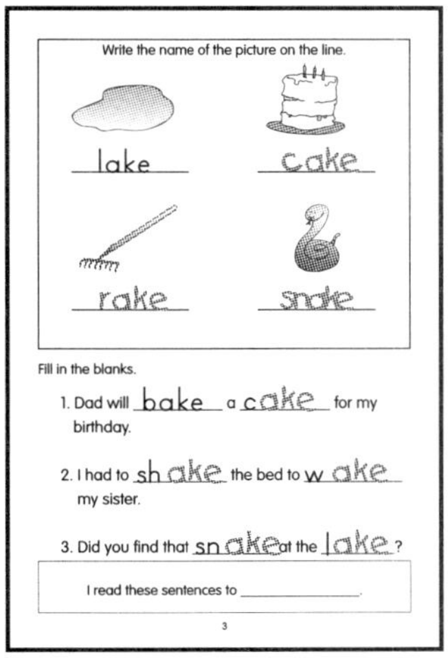
Write the name of the picture on the line.

lake cake

rake snake

Fill in the blanks.

1. Dad will bake a cake for my birthday.

2. I had to shake the bed to wake my sister.

3. Did you find that snake at the lake?

I read these sentences to ________.

3

page 4

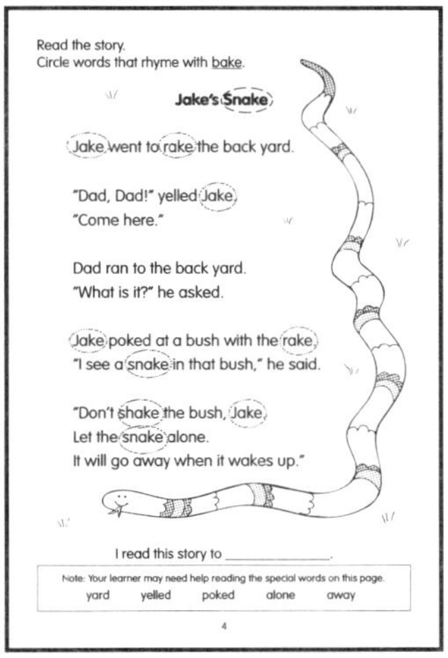
Read the story.
Circle words that rhyme with bake.

Jake's Snake

Jake went to rake the back yard.

"Dad, Dad!" yelled Jake.
"Come here."

Dad ran to the back yard.
"What is it?" he asked.

Jake poked at a bush with the rake.
"I see a snake in that bush," he said.

"Don't shake the bush, Jake.
Let the snake alone.
It will go away when it wakes up."

I read this story to ________.

Note: Your learner may need help reading the special words on this page.
yard yelled poked alone away

4

page 6

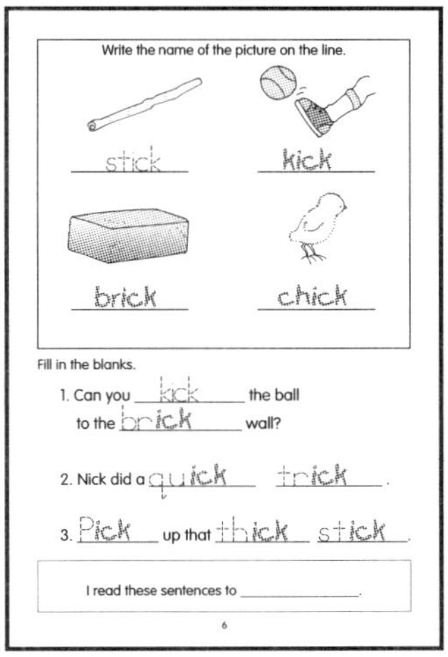
Write the name of the picture on the line.

stick kick

brick chick

Fill in the blanks.

1. Can you kick the ball to the brick wall?

2. Nick did a quick trick.

3. Pick up that thick stick.

I read these sentences to ________.

6

page 7

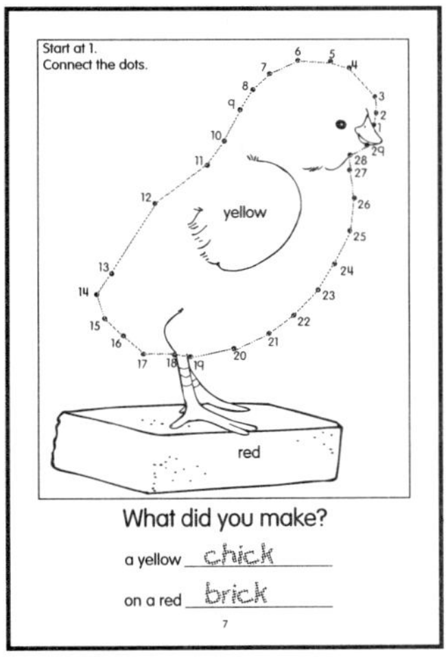
Start at 1.
Connect the dots.

yellow

red

What did you make?

a yellow chick

on a red brick

7

page 8

Read the story.
Put a line under words that rhyme with kick.

Nick's Chick

Nick was sick.
He had to stay in bed.

Mom got Nick a trick chick on a stick.
The chick went "click, click, click"
as it ran up and down the stick.

The funny chick made Nick feel better.

I read this story to ________.

Note: Your learner may need help reading the special words on this page.
stay funny better down feel

8

page 10

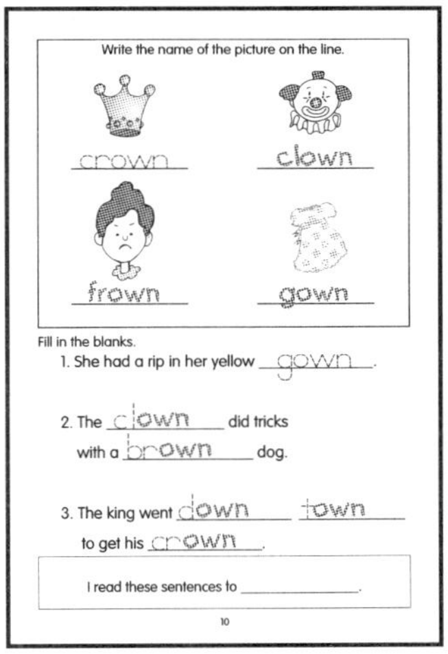
Write the name of the picture on the line.

crown clown

frown gown

Fill in the blanks.

1. She had a rip in her yellow gown.

2. The clown did tricks with a brown dog.

3. The king went down town to get his crown.

I read these sentences to ________.

10

page 11

Read the story.
Put an X on the words that rhyme with down.

The Sad King

"The king is not happy.
See that big frown.
What can we do to make him smile?"
asked the queen.

"I saw a clown when I was downtown,"
said the prince.
We can get her to make the king smile."

The clown came in a funny, brown gown.
She did tricks for the king.

"I will not frown now," said the king.
"I like the tricks you did."
And the king gave the clown his crown.

I read this story to ________.

Note: Your learner may need help reading the special words on this page.
happy smile asked prince king queen

11

page 13

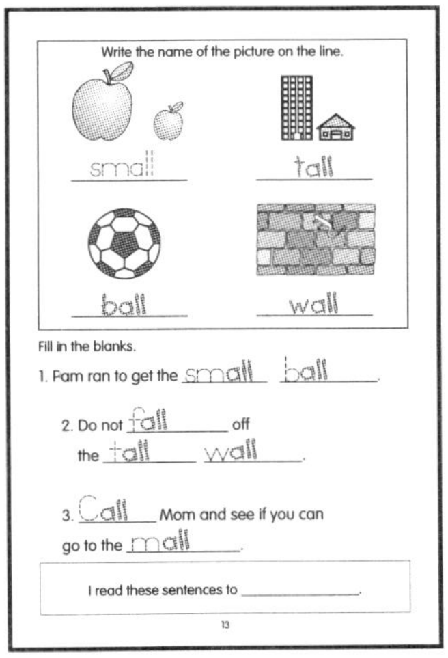
Write the name of the picture on the line.

small tall

ball wall

Fill in the blanks.

1. Fam ran to get the small ball.

2. Do not fall off the tall wall.

3. Call Mom and see if you can go to the mall.

I read these sentences to ________.

13

page 14

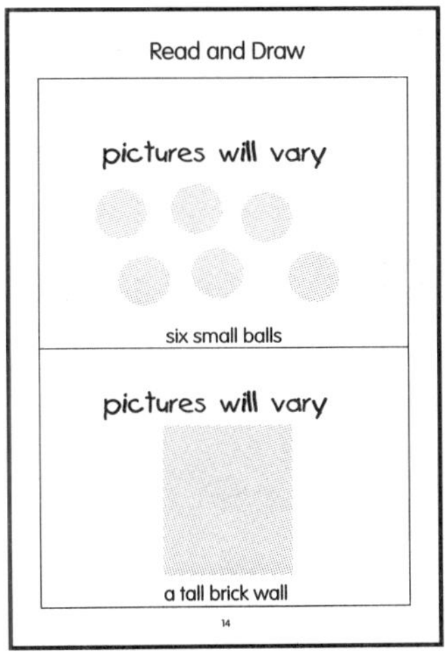
Read and Draw

pictures will vary

six small balls

pictures will vary

a tall brick wall

14

page 15

Read the story.
Look for the words that rhyme with all.

The Best Gift

Kate went to the mall to get a gift for her small brother.
She was looking for the best gift.

Kate looked in each stall up and down the hall.
She went in and out of the toy and gift shops.

At last she gave a big call, "I will get him that ball!
He will like to bounce it on the tall wall at the park."

Write the words in the story that rhyme with all.

mall	call
small	ball
stall	tall
hall	wall

I read this story to ________________.

Note: Your learner may need help reading the special words on this page.
brother toy bounce looked gift shops

15

page 17

Write the name of the picture on the line.

jay

tray

gray

hay

Fill in the blanks.

1. Ray made a jay out of clay.
2. Will you stay and play with me?
3. I saw a gray whale in the bay.

I read these sentences to ________________.

17

page 18

Read the story.
Put a circle around the words that rhyme with day.

A Gray Jay

Jay wanted to go out and play.
It was a cold, gray day.
"You have to stay inside today," said his mother.

Jay sat and looked outside.
He saw a blue jay in the tree.
"I will make that jay with my clay," he said.

He did not have blue clay so he made a gray jay.
"That is just the way I want it to look," said Jay.

Just then a ray of sunshine came in.
"You can go out now," called his mother.

Jay put the gray jay on a tray.
He set it on his desk.
He ran out into the sunshine to play.

I read this story to ________________.

Note: Your learner may need help reading the special words on this page.
wanted inside sunshine cold outside looked

18

page 20

Write the name of the picture on the line.

sky

spy

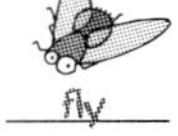
fly

cry

Fill in the blanks.

1. Why is he so shy?
2. Can you fly your kite in the sky?
3. Don't cry. I will try to help you.

I read these sentences to ________________.

20

page 21

Start at 1.
Connect the dots.

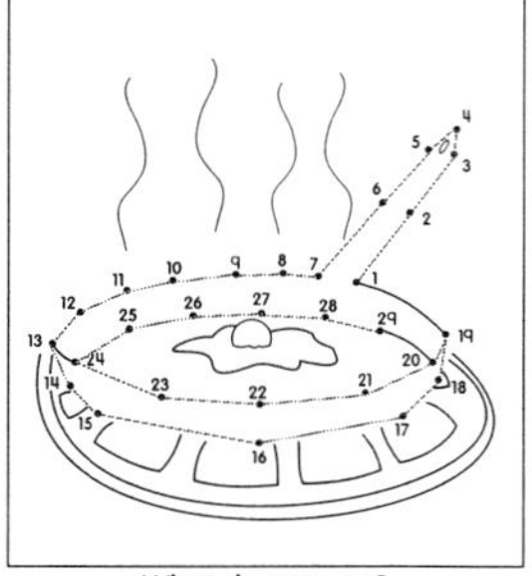

What do you see?

an egg in a fry ing pan

21

page 22

Read the story.
Put an X on all of the words that rhyme with my.

Up in a Tree

The small boy wanted to fly his plane.
"I will try to get it up in the sky," he said.
He saw the plane fly. Then it hit a tree.
He started to cry.

A big girl came by. "Don't cry," she said.
"I will try to get the plane."
She went up the tree and got the plane.

"Here it is," she said.
"Why don't you fly it away from the tree."

"Thank you," said the shy boy.

I read this story to ________________.

Note: Your learner may need help reading the special words on this page.
wanted Don't from started away thank

22

page 24

Write the name of the picture on the line.

bell

well

shell

Fill in the blanks.

1. Yell when you smell the cake.
2. Can you spell shell?
3. The bell fell down the well.

I read these sentences to ________________.

24

page 25

Read the story.
Circle the words that rhyme with bell.

What a Smell!

Ring the bell.
Give a yell.
Run and tell.
A skunk just squirted my pup.

Mr. Fell,
What do you sell
To get rid of the smell?
Can you clean him up?

I read this story to ________________.

Note: Your learner may need help reading the special words on this page.
squirted clean give Mr.

25

page 27

Write the name of the picture on the line.

night

light

knight

Fill in the blanks.

1. Todd saw a bright light last night.
2. Is it right to get in a fight?
3. The plane flight will start right here.

I read these sentences to ________________.

27

page 28

Read and Draw

pictures will vary

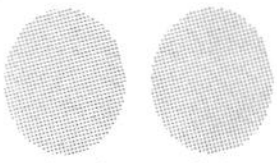

knights in a fight

pictures will vary

a bright light

pictures will vary

a dark night

28

page 29

Read the story.
Put an X on the words that rhyme with light.

A Fright in the Night

A knight was going back to the castle.
It was very late on a very dark night.
Suddenly he saw a bright light far off.
"What was that?" he said.
"I must get closer so I can see."

The knight got a bad fright.
The light had come from a huge dragon.
"What am I going to do?" said the knight.
"I don't want to fight a dragon tonight."

Just then the dragon took flight.
The knight did not have to fight that night.

I read this story to ________________.

Note: Your learner may need help reading the special words on this page.
castle closer took huge suddenly dragon

29

page 30

Write Rhyming Words

Words will vary.

cake	rake	make
sick	pick	trick
down	brown	town
ball	hall	wall
may	play	stay
fly	by	cry
back	tack	sack
ball	call	hall
night	light	right

30